This book belongs to

_____

Copyright © 2020 by APPLE PARKER PUBLISHING, LLC
Printed in the United States of America

All rights reserved. This book or portions thereof may not be reproduced or transmitted in any form or by any means -- electronic, mechanical, photocopying, recording, or otherwise without the prior written permission of the authors.
ISBN: 978-1-7334373-1-8

Written with the help of Michelle Grier, Just Write 4 Kids LLC
Illustrations by Reginald Byers

It was a lovely spring school-day and
Apple and Leah were super excited!
They couldn't wait for Spring break to begin.
They were singing with joy,
"We lo-o-o-o-ve Spring break".

When they walked into their classroom, Apple and Leah began to worry.

They wondered why their favorite teacher wasn't at the door greeting the students.

"Where is Ms. Perkins?"

They became very sad that Spring break was near, and Ms. Perkins wasn't there to help them celebrate.

All of a sudden, someone walked in
and stood over the desks.
They were all shocked.

It was Mrs. Jordan, the teacher
that never smiles.

She is very tall, almost as tall
as the flagpole outside.

As always, Mrs. Jordan was frowning.

Right after she walked in she shouted,
"OPEN YOUR NOTEBOOKS!"

The students didn't have any joy because they wished that Ms. Perkins would walk in.

But, to their surprise, Ms. Perkins arrived.
They were so delighted to see
her smiling face.

The students closed their books and
ran as fast as they could
to Ms. Perkins.

She kindly said,
"No running in the classroom".

Apple quickly looked at Leah and said,
"Maybe we should just be patient".
They decided to wait for the
class to settle down before asking
Ms. Perkins a question.

After everyone returned to their seats, Ms. Perkins thanked Mrs. Jordan for staying with her students.

Leah raised her hand.
Ms. Perkins called Leah's name.
She asked, "Where were you earlier?"
Ms. Perkins just smiled.

She stepped out of the classroom, then returned with a tray of cupcakes.

Mrs. Jordan stayed with their class while Ms. Perkins picked up their Spring break surprise from the bakery.

She is the sweetest teacher ever.

I dedicate this book to my
WONDERFUL FAMILY.
I LOVE YOU!

Check out more of

The Series

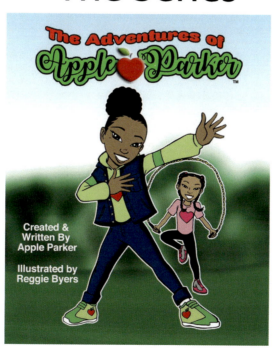

Made in the USA
Monee, IL
10 December 2020